NERVOUS
SYSTEM

NERVOUS SYSTEM

Poems

ROSALIE MOFFETT

ecco

An Imprint of HarperCollinsPublishers

Page 77 serves as a continuation of the copyright page.

NERVOUS SYSTEM. Copyright © 2019 by Rosalie Moffett. All rights reserved. Printed in the United States of America. No part of this book may be used or reproduced in any manner whatsoever without written permission except in the case of brief quotations embodied in critical articles and reviews. For information, address HarperCollins Publishers, 195 Broadway, New York, NY 10007.

HarperCollins books may be purchased for educational, business, or sales promotional use. For information, please email the Special Markets Department at SPsales@harpercollins.com.

FIRST EDITION

Designed by Renata De Oliveira

Library of Congress Cataloging-in-Publication Data has been applied for.

ISBN 978-0-06-293021-7

19 20 21 22 23 LSC 10 9 8 7 6 5 4 3 2 1

For my mother

CONTENTS

NERVOUS
SYSTEM

What the Mind Makes

I close in
on the room where she's been
        long forgotten, long

hair loose around her face, her
        mind's sky eye-blue,
a quiet brain-full of sun. My camera

        floats the hospital hall
and my memory grows, rising dough, it self-
        fabricates, zooms

out to include in the frame the necklace
        of cars fleeing the storm,
child-me asleep in one glinting bead.

        These images arrive, file
themselves in the folder with the others
        marked *mother.*

I don't trust them, don't claim much
        for accuracy, though
there is a bit of faith

        in what the mind makes
for itself, isn't there? Filling in
        what isn't there—

Nervous System

It's the one where the wolf
spider's silk sac is separated from her. The eggs,
removed, are replaced

with small lead shot. Mute, round changelings.
They're returned
to the spider. She can be described as frantic.

She struggles to lift them,
to hurry away. Subsequent experiments
show, with heavier loads,

she will break even
her legs, so
intent is she on reclaiming

what's hers.

Scientist's betrayal
of sympathy, my mother described this to me.
        She held spiders

in such high regard, how could I not sorrow
        for the spider-mother? Little Miss Muffet
they called me, but I was never afraid, never

        when I was little. When it hit me,
I was grown: fear my mother would forget me, one copy
        of my self deleted,

leaden shape
        in her mind
where I once was.

She studied snails
on a bit-spit of land in the ocean. Bright midday
        she hit her head, battered it to a black pool

of wordlessness. To dream
        you are bitten by a spider reveals a conflict
with your mother. To dream of a snail

        suggests a spiraling inwards
for answers. The concussion made a shell, cool well
        of clues inside a hurricane

-emptied hospital. In the myth, a spider
        thought the world
into existence. She threw her dew-dropped web

        into the sky and made the stars.
In her mechanical bed, my mother relearned the names
        for things—*flood, daughter, glove*—lights

flickering on in her planetarium.

Seeing stars, it's called
when the brain collides with the skull or spins
          in its dish. This, with

a ringing like what, when shaken, the dead
          lightbulb makes.
Eruption of brights, sparklers

          of neurotransmitters
dazzling all at once: flashy finale
          of a town's last Fourth of July

before the mill leaves or the dam is built—
Concussion, a word, easy
to confuse with *percussion*, the crash cymbal

          shattering the air
in cartoons, as when Wile E. Coyote drops an anvil
          on what turns out to be

himself and the stars appear, wreathe
          his head with their
catastrophe.

I was taught the lyric is a song
          outside of time.
In narrative, there is consequence:

          A leads to B. Before
she hit her head she'd been watching
          the snails heal themselves, tricks

their brains performed on the stage
          the microscope made.
Once, as a child, I helped, wielding tiny scissors,

          knife-sharp, to snip
one eye off each snail and she recorded how
          the brain ordered

the eye to regenerate. Because of her,
          I knew it was *eye stalk,*
not antenna, not tentacle.

          I knew all the right terms.
I wasn't allowed to retain a childish lexicon.
          On the playground,

I'd tell the girls with kickballs wedged
          under their shirts, *It's called
a uterus*— Since then, I've learned

          the word *sequela,* as in
sequel, as in symptoms that follow
          a concussion

like an army, erecting black tents
   in the mind. I've ceased
to believe a song can exist

   for very long
outside repercussion.

Seeing stars—as if in awe—as if driven
into the country, moonless night, for this purpose.
        Each year, the meteor shower

reminds how the brain hankers after pattern.
        How, after each shooting star,
the decision: keep looking there or at another

                quadrant of sky? We didn't have to
drive out into the country. We were already here,
        my mother and I, with the dogs,

the coop of blinking chickens, the log-ringed lake,
        which is really a river, dammed,
next to which they collected the wolf spiders

                to see what they could carry. It wasn't
about strength, per se, but about *load-bearing gait*.
        I was raised to believe anything

learned can be used, and just look at us now:
        the way she moves
under the new regime

                of her body. Bewildered,
the spiders might have wondered why they couldn't
        lift what, before,

had been easy, and my mother
        can look around—
everything appears the same: same brown

eggs in a carton, a peach
halved on the cutting board, blood-colored pit
stuck tight. Same fight as always

to pull it out. The old awe, making its fever
of sun, hiding the stars
in its empty sky.

So out-in-the-middle-of-nowhere, that there
        was, growing up, a certain kind of time
spent with myself. At night the textured ceiling

        would not stop turning
itself into faces—the slightest suggestion of a presence
        became a presence. A conversation

of language-like noise could be had,
        given enough rocks
to throw, one after another, into the creek:

        a show of how the mind
metabolized its craw of sound. It made perfect sense
        to learn that spiders have

"book lungs." Small flare of kinship: image
        meaning words might make up a life
stuff, a kind of atmosphere.

        What the brain breathes.
New words opened new rooms of myself
        to myself. Looking up, after her

appointment, *aphasia*, swung wide
        a door to a black hole
my mind inched away from.

She made two of me—twins, of which
        only I survived, which is why
she doubled me again

        every time I left the house,
saying, *Take care of Rosi*, as if one of me
        could watch over another of me.

There are many things one can make seem
        to happen with words.
I felt I was being followed

        by the faithful dog of myself, as if
I had stepped half out of my body.
        Little perfections exist.

For instance, that *by myself* endures
        in clear opposition
to *alone*. It is possible

        to be content
like this. It is impossible to imagine
        how to go about thinking

in the absence of language.

After a head trauma, distance
is one measurement of injury: across small breaks,
        the nerves regrow.

Spanning large gaps requires silk grafts:
        spider threads
ensheathed in nerve cells, new suspension bridges

        between the word *flood* and the rush
of rising seawater. This science reveals the body
        sees the silk as kindred,

absorbs it, so there is no ensuing infection.
        It is easy to imagine the brain
as a meshwork of silk rope bridges,

        perhaps easier as a city or a field of grass.
A lone apricot tree, its orange fruits flaming up
        like ideas—

Some trees grow so heavy they split
        from the weight
of their fruit. Who's to say what we'll yield

        to? Too many blossoms. *Flowers
are the earth laughing*, said the florist's window.
        I can trust any entity

that funnels its resources into a mess
        of petals as a hedging of bets
against what might get lost

        given frost or high wind. Is it
a desperate laughter? Me, her only daughter,
        fought for, against

her own body which shed two others
        who might've become me
except they never did. It's called

        June drop when a tree tries
to rid itself of too many, for instance, peaches.
        Every sweet thing you buy

in the store has come far from a ritual
        suffering to meet you
in the fluorescence.

Perhaps I have no business
imagining her brain, dawdling in a picture.
        It doesn't matter

how many times I make the metaphor
        if I am no real witch,
no powers of transformation to save her,

        the one who might be
content as an apricot tree. The scientists are still
        working their magic

to take silk grafts beyond the test phase. I am here, morning
        after morning, writing *my mother is
perennial, is wintering over,*

        *a trick birthday candle,
a pylon, my mother
        is the spider, breaking herself—*

Perhaps it wasn't her head hitting the rocks
           after all. She, dyslexic
all along, knew the painstaking worlds

           in the words whose marks
were off, installed backwards
           or upside down.

Less electricity in the language
           parts of the brain, this
makes the dyslexic

           identifiable in the MRI.
I've drawn a brightly lit mansion in which a very small
           version of my mother

sleeps on a velvet sofa in a dark library.
           I've drawn a lot of pictures
because it's hard for me to believe

           in anything
that hasn't been made
           into something else.

Who was it who said
The word is the only door
        through which a thought

can pass? It sprints, two at a time,
        the escalator of the throat. Oh,
of course there are paintings,

        music. Of course, at all times,
what's under wants to rise up, out.
        But what I mean

is not what's labored over,
        not watercolor, not
vibrato. Instead: what happens

        in the morning
when a ceramic coffee cup, the one she loves,
        with its blue flower, slips

from her hand, shatters on the tiles
        and racing up to my mouth,
lightning, comes—

We played a game on the bus that took us
        to soccer matches
and tennis tournaments, a game at which now

        I would excel. The key was never
to be tricked into giving an answer; the trick
        was to parry with questions.

E.g., *Who do you have a crush on?* To which,
        Why do you care? And then,
Are you worried we'll laugh? Etc. If you took too long,

        you were out.
The cheddar-colored bus carried us in the dark
        through rolling hills,

back to the high school, and then I had my own
        drive home through more night
and more fields. She'd be there,

        washing her hair or snapping beans.
We'd been playing the game for months. The question:
        What's wrong

with you? hung in the air
        like dust we could see
only in certain angles of light. To think of having

        so many answers
you might give one out
        by mistake—

Faced with one of those holy moments
        where light strikes
a misted web, fires it up like a neon sign

        advertising how the world's been
triple-majoring in Grandeur,
        Fear and Leisure Studies for years,

someone had a bright idea for wringing a little more
        music from it. Thousands
of strands of dragline silk

        from yellow orb weavers
were twisted to create violin strings
        stronger than steel,

a *soft and profound timbre*. The Tchaikovsky
        emanating from them—you can
hear it, a sound the spider

        never intended.

I started out looking
　　　　like her; she cut
my hair like hers; my face was like hers.

　　　　And then I underwent
a phase where I appeared as someone else,
　　　　though now the older

I get, the more again I begin to resemble
　　　　my mother. My father
and I discuss whether the way

　　　　her mind flounders
might be genetic, inheritable, and he, all doom
　　　　-and-gloom, concludes

it likely is, and may have nothing
　　　　to do with her brain
colliding with the inside of her skull

　　　　so many years ago and so
I feel around inside my head for soft spots
　　　　that might turn

worse. Some fruits get one little ding
　　　　and a day later are miserable
all over, collapsed and black.

I am at the ballet, watching a woman
         dance herself to death
to ensure spring will come again.

         In the parking lot, snow
is growing grimier. My father is leaving his voice
         in my silenced phone.

My mother is at the kitchen table, frozen
         bags of homegrown peas
scattered around her,

         all bloodied as they melted
against her head. The thing with her brain
         makes her balance go.

Later, she stole the stapler the nurse used
         to pull the cut shut
because what if she should

         need it again? *I have to stop working,*
my father is saying in the message, *I can't*
         leave her at home alone.

The music is crashing to a halt, so abrupt it was said
         to suddenly fall over on its side.
Stravinsky disparaged his final chord as *a noise,*

but could not write anything
better for the end. I have dressed up for the ballet
in something borrowed

from my mother's closet and never returned: black,
strapless, with tumbling
white flowers—

Up early for the long drive home, I become
        aware of the orb weavers' webs
built between parallel power lines—

        they gleam in the streetlamp, beaded
with what looks like their own tiny orb-lights, solar systems
        strung around the flickering white.

All those moths roving dumbly toward the ersatz
        moon, their navigation
gummed up with the modern world, and the spiders,

        feasting, clinging between
the spiral-bound wires, the electricity—and me,
        pre-coffee, dumbstruck in the brown-dark.

Human voltage is everything. It's our hurt, traveling
        to the brain, it's our heart, in fear
quickening its pace. This electricity, lineless,

        jumps cell to cell—
each cell, like a castle, flings up its portcullis, potassium
        gets out, sodium gets in,

and this mix creates a charge that blasts ajar
        the next door, chain reaction
that takes the spark where it needs to go.

        I need to understand this, standing
under the webs between the wires, because I can see her
        better if I can see into her:

electricity gone berserk, wrong turns
        tugging her body
into its spasms, rickety system flashing

        with pain and information. I'm prone
to think of it among the still shapes of early morning,
        the spiders in their jeweled

territories, the power lines taking electricity to the TVs,
        the toasters and coffeemakers, everything
about to wake up.

The *arachnoid mater* is translated
　　　　as spider mother, or mother
in the image of a spider.

　　　　It is the middle
of three membranes covering the brain,
　　　　so named for its silk

-like fibers, delicate, reaching into the inner
　　　　layer, the one closest
to the brain: the *pia mater*

　　　　the tender mother.

To protect itself, a jumping spider will secure
          a tether to whatever
it's standing on, a silk

          filament so, failing a jump,
it's saved from a fall. It does this all the time,
          in fact. If shaken

from a leaf, it can simply return
          to the leaf. Every time I call, I peer
through the opening her voice makes

          in the barrier
of distance between us. Spiders are good
          at survival,

they manage in arctic, desert, cave.
          They've prevailed
because they sense so well what wants

          to come for them.
In the dark, with the smooth surface
          against my cheek,

I listen to her. Whether, in this,
          I tend to a tether
home or apprehend what's coming

          for me, it doesn't matter
or it's the same thing—

In the womb we watch our eyelids. This is enough
        to blaze a pathway
in the brain, wiring it in anticipation

        of light. A warm-up act.
The neurologist says, *The world must be dreamed
        before it can be seen*—

Which has its pithy ring. But of what, these dreams?
        The brain doesn't need much
of the world, it seems—restless visual cortex

        rehearsing in the mind's
dark theater. What does that do—
        what does it do

to write this? Field of tall grass, ventured through.
        Catalog of damage, pre-fathomed
as practice, to the one who once shielded me

        in her body
like a lit match. How she glows
        now in the MRI, does not give up

the secret of her brain's fumble for words,
        or her spasms
like a Mexican jumping bean. I can't get that

        phrase out of my mind.
I know now what hides, what jumps: larva,
        blind inside the bean,

jolts in the heat of the palm, chews
          a hole in the bean's husk
and seals it up with silk. Next, a moth, mouthless,

          it'll just butt its way out,
new into the world of air we must assume
          it has foreseen.

But what do I divine about what transformation
          comes next, given her mouth,
wordless, and the way the air

          seems to reach out
and shake her?

The diving bell spider
spends its life underwater in balloons
        made from two silk sheets

sealed and filled with air
        brought down in bubbles
from the surface. What must it be like

        to be the sole crosser
of thresholds? The balloon breathes
        like a gill.

The spider encounters
        only its own kind
of spider down there.

        What if it's like water,
the afterlife, a world
        alongside ours?

Some of the smallest
spiders use their silk to go ballooning—
        i.e., they release

a few gossamer strands into the air
        and are carried away
by rising currents.

        This is how they colonized
islands, were discovered in the sails of ships
        that hadn't seen land

for days. Who's to save me from looking
        all day online at painless ways to move
through the world? Who's to blame

        for the way she's ended up? Imagine
being so negligible in the eyes
        of gravity, that the earth

has barely a hold on you.

It's not one spindle, one spool of thread,
          unreeling into a web—
a spinneret, instead, is a set of microscopic spigots

          releasing each its own filament
and the spider has a multiplex of spinnerets
          which work in concert or solo

to spin various weights, array of specific silks.
          So, a remarkable factory
spends its life by the bathroom mirror

          where my face appears.
How easy it is to miss this
          world we've been allowed into.

The inside of her, so
mysterious no one can figure or fix it. Aquarius
        is said to be a wanderer, scientist,

a stubborn free spirit, but my mother is concerned
        with the heavens
only when they cough up their weird auroras,

        their summer meteor showers.
The vagus nerve is named for the way it vagabonds
        about the body. The largest nerve

in the nervous system, it's responsible
        for controlling the heart,
the stomach, tears, for *salvation*—

        I suppose it is supposed to be
salivation. So close, though, the ideas
        intertwine, twin—

Inside her, with their robotic snake
            they snapped pictures, tourists in a cave.
Did what anyone too long in a delicate place

            ends up doing. Their snake scraped up
her long, vagabonding nerve, so she can't eat much
            anymore, just liquid. Her heaven:

tomatoes, rows of bush beans, melons, her tangle
            of salvation, idle. *It's a shame
she's not a spider, can't sink in her fangs,*

            liquefy food from the inside, I say
aloud in the room where I found the black widow
            trapped between the window

and the screen. Not sure how to kill her
            or let her go,
I left her there. Nothing at all

            to prey on, slim ambit
of movement, I marvel
            she endures.

Her blood so thin when they drew it
          her arm grew itself a blue-black
blotch, huge. *Too much*

          aspirin. The body in pain
needs venom. The brain, mass of castle-cells,
          has pain-only traffic routes:

ache and pang and sting travel on channels
          velvet tarantula toxin
can block. *To dream you are bitten by a spider*

          reveals a conflict
with your mother—but think of the dream,
          the idea of a spider

the brain waves like a flare, a little request
          for venom, a little
like my mother: her blue arm, her self

          which held my self, idea
of me, until it was real.

It's misleading, isn't it, the *revelation*
             of a conflict. My mother
and I are peculiar

             in our closeness, so
it can't be that is what I'm thinking,
             positioned, as I am

at her table as she holds her hands
             up, saying *At least they haven't gotten worse—*
meaning arthritis, now that she's off all the blood

             -thinning painkillers. Though
she tossed an artillery of orange
             pill bottles, she kept

the oxycodone, the hydrocodone and codeine
             in their cabinet altar
in case things get worse, meaning

             not her hands, but how
when my dog was on his last legs, I longed
             to spare him the vet

he was afraid of, to give him something sleepy
             myself: float him over the edge.
I'd heard, for instance, of this stick-on

             morphine patch—*You'll know,*
I was told, *when it's time,* but I think
             I was a little late. *Just hit me over the head*

when I get too gone, she used to say. So OK, it is a conflict
      between the me who's been
smoothing a spot in my mind for years, like a dog

      turning in circles
and the me who's afraid of living
      without a mother. Each of us

some night will visit an innermost cabinet
      and find no cache
of anything to make it easier.

Her checked bag was crammed
with raspberry starts yanked up the morning
                she flew out

so I could, upon her arrival, right
                away, stick them in the ground.
A more convincing living

                connection to the home I might
one day return to on the occasion
                of her death, whereupon

I would live with the originals,
                what gave rise to the progeny
I've loved and willed into the thin red soil

                of my city yard: the irises,
the portulaca and lavender. Back in the canyon,
                I would be returned

to all the mothers whose purpose
                is to multiply—by rhizomes
and burrs, canes and runners—except

                of course, mine. Whereupon
I would be standing in the garden.
                It would be spring

and things would be blooming
                like crazy, as if they
had pulled everything

                they needed from the ground,
took it from the sun and air.

I see a woman walking a dog—see from afar
        a woman walking her dog.
But closer, it's a lawn mower,

        not a dog
trotting ahead of her: life's little bait
        and switch. What I thought

could be thought of as alive, soul-bound,
        (whatever it means to think
it feels) turns out to be a contraption, indefinitely

        repairable. It does not speak,
does not whimper. It doesn't take much
        to look at her

small sweat-beads, squint pulled
        like a visor, and see
an elaborate machine

        pushing an obedient animal—
These perforations in the story we tell
        make it easy

to tear the self in two.
        I.e., see how I pass the time,
pleasantly, with the apparatus

        of my body, keeping it
company, like a girl with a doll.
        Crouching, I rest

my hand on the mower's
        head, warm and shuddering
from its combustion.

I return to the idea
like the shape I wake each day into,
      of the spider breaking her legs

when I feel ugly, but strong. Silver lining is thinking
      I won't break.
My mother's ballerina genes, in me

      were drowned
by my father's sturdiness. Lately, a study
      of twin sisters

found the one with greater leg strength held on
      to her mind
better as she aged—so there are two

      silver linings, i.e., there begins
to be a material like the shiny insulation I wore
      a mask to handle, and gloves.

The pamphlet in the plane's seat back
      tells me gratitude
is like a muscle you can beef up

      with practice,
so I practice until I am muffled with silver
      fiberglass linings. Something

digs at my layers, wants to get in
      to say *No*
you and your mind were made

      by your mother and look
at her now.

In fact, I've never fractured, though I've flown
            many times through air,
landed hard on the ground. Heartbroken

            and silly, yes, but my bones've
held. Hers, a little birdish, shifted
            around, some vertebrae

slipped sideways in their tower.
            This was after she lifted
all those buckets of rocks and concrete

            up the metal scaffolds.
She wanted us to build, ourselves, the house
            we lived in. The thick walls kept us

from the fire that licked up the canyon,
            charred the graceful summer
grass into nothing. So those rocks

            were, perhaps, worth it.
She, reinforced now with metal rods.
            For everything the spiders have

to offer, she's been born or hurt
            too early: the nerve graphs,
the pain-relief toxins,

            the spider-silk screws
which flex like the bones
            they're in.

Why, people ask even now
        in disgust,
spiders? But that was how you could tell

        I was my mother's
child—unafraid
        to cup them in my hands,

to ferry them out-of-doors while other girls
        made up their minds
that I would not be their friend. Her world

        was largely harmless, marvelous, each moving
bit of it not a threat but a wonder. The mother
        I know is the mother

who hit her head or who suffers
        from something that'll come for me.
I am gentle, patient, easy to awe. This goodness I got

        from her is bound
to be yoked to a curse—no bargain
        is so good.

How does the saying go? *They're cut
        from the same cloth*—though
this thing about spiderweb, how it could be used

      to stitch up a brain's tears, mend me,
means I might go about unafraid, unbothered.
      I must've blundered

through a thousand perfect works
      of silk, resplendent with dew
and light I didn't see in time.

It seems I should know what it is
            like to be her, cut,
as we are, from the same cloth, having drunk

            for years the same water,
which now I know is not what water tastes like
            everywhere, from our well,

and having taken in our scenery as a kind
            of sustenance. Home
at night I heard the hollow sound of logs

            jockeying at the shore of the lake which was
not a lake, but a river, whose dam had turbines
            churning in the dark

under water to send power loping
            across fields to the town
where rooms were filled with light washing

            over the faces of people
watching other lives. Meanwhile, it was beautiful,
            she said, to live

at the edge of the idea
            of a place. A smooth surface
to look across and beneath it something

            you imagined
happening: roads and men or women entering
            or leaving houses, a dog

yawning, baskets and baskets of apricots
        hoisted into the steamboats
anchored on the swift river

        under what the river
had now become. Are we both not made a little
        of this world we spent such time

envisioning—which is to say
        a little nonexistent?

It's called *sweetening*
when laugh tracks are added to soap operas,
            so that sense that what you saw

was seen, too, by others was thought
            to have a taste to it. The canyon
I lived in was empty, no FM, no TV,

            so the lives we watched were ours,
or they were ones that struck like dreams
            when we bit into apricots

we picked from trees whose fruits had floated
            when the river was dammed,
their pits arriving at the shore of land that later

            became ours.
When she saw the canyon, her face lit up.
            It's perfect. I want it.

The border to a place, disappeared—
            What could *it* be except
a landscape to look at when she was looking in?

            The way certain people might turn
over and over to a blank page,
            might make it full.

Aspirin, ibuprofen, hydrocodone—
          little rattle of rhythm
in the bottle, little shake. *With food*, they say

          so, food, a comfort
these days, the days like soap chips, dissolving
          into evening. The radio on,

on and on. The dogs gallop through the hills' old snow, still
          reveling in the way it's changed
the way the world feels.

          Inside, my mother's left
two house spiders in the corner of the shower.
          She's left them all

over the house, clinging in the tall ceilings. Stupid city
          architect didn't know
what it was to live in this dust-tunnel, this canyon:

          up in the eaves, streamers
and streamers of dirty cobwebs and the smoke
          detector. Puffs of wing-dust

shuffled from moths drawn to its tiny green light
          set it off: alarms
all night some nights, nothing

          to be done, the small button
to quiet the sound, round, white like a pill, visible
          but out of reach.

It appears and appears to me,
        the world, every time
I open my eyes. It is loyal

        or it is just
doing its job.
        It makes its walls

of rain, cups us in its
        enclosures
of fog. When she pulls up

        a fistful
of watercress from the hole
        in the creek ice,

there is a shock of life
        in the roots—small
snails, caddis fly larvae in their pebble

        sleeping bags,
knowing now a new bit of raw
        air, a breeze. Nowhere

else do we exist. My mother's cold
        -red fingers, picking
the snails from the root-tangle,

        holding them up
in the thin light to her eye, her joy—
        nowhere else.

This must be what we agreed on,
        when we agreed to come
into being.

My mother's dog is buried under a railroad tie
        in the garden
because if there's not something heavy

        there, something quiet
will come and dig it up. My dog was cremated
        because I wanted to bury him

but where in my rented city yard
        could I? *I hope you know*
I'm donating my body to science. I'm about as far

        as I can go and be
in the same country as my mother,
        who is almost at the end

of the winding highway connecting the town
        to *nowhere*:
a hollowed canyon and its black cows, its river

        enameled with whatever
light the time of day is making. As soon as I held
        the dog's expensive ashes,

I knew it was an absurd question,
        where he'd want to be
scattered—couldn't walk myself

        through his dog-logic,
his trying to grasp what it mattered what I did
        with his body when he was

no longer in it. *Who knows what, then,*
         they'll learn about me,
what a specimen I'll be. The country is vast.

         I left home, drove away
towing a U-Haul. The world is full
         of beauty, is enormous.

It doesn't make a bit of difference
         where I put any
of the ones I've loved.

Before the dam,
there'd been, under way, a dig
        unearthing bit by bit

a prehistoric human whose bones would give
        some sense of who we were
before we were us.

        When the river rose,
the water seeped up through the porous ground
        the way the scientists warned it would,

and the bones disappeared. It happens
        so often, that feeling
of being on the very edge

        of realizing something, almost
as if remembering it: bright spark in the mind's
        breeze—but the flitting movement

of a bat, the exhale of a train
        reverberating up the canyon,
that twitch-aside of attention—

        Then, whatever it was:
gone, sunk. And over the surface, small Jet Skis
        trailing wakes, elegant lines traveling

toward the makeshift shore
        where they piled all the gravel
they'd blasted out.

Again, on the phone, I
turn to the familiar idea: if she, ghostlike,
        climbed into me,

like sharing a car or as if I folded
        up so tightly
in the dresser drawer of my self

        that she could fit
there too—and then I'd dive from the dock
        into the river, or dance or hoist

a bucket of peaches, all
        the while, she'd be thrilled,
so free of the sharp

        or crippling or shooting or dull
or whatever other blunt modifiers
        there are for pain.

If, in a dream I open a book, I find the words
        in some alien language.
Same when a hurricane churns toward me:

        over and over, I turn
to the Doppler map, no sense for the marks or colors.
        Given a student with a fervor

for preserving nature, I always ask
        What's the most effective thing
you can do alone? Recycle, some say, no meat—

        The stock answer is *vote,* though
the real thing to reduce your carbon footprint
        is to never have children.

My mother' genes, in me, it's fair to say,
        are languishing,
but what can you do

        alone? Turn the radio on
and the voice gives way to the robot groan
        and empty dial tone

of the storm warning. I guess all agree
        in such times to take a break
from language. I take a rope

and pull the limbs
that'll come, dead, off the tree. I fill
the gas tank, the water jug,

climb in the claw-foot and pass the time
singing in the odd
acoustics, that comforting blur

the tub makes of my words.

To dream of a storm
reveals a fear of losing control. To dream
        you are in the eye of a storm

means the loss is irreversible. A lemon tree
        means it's winter
in America and a truck has crashed. To hear of this

        through the small speaker of the cell phone
means, in your dream, a woman is kneeling
        in her mother's garden, setting mousetraps.

In the real world: a snap of light and a bunch of white
        shines through an MRI.
(What is it, pulls back, clicks

        precariously in the mind?)
If, when awake, you see a radiologist sigh,
        it means you are in the eye: swirl, like a skirt

of storm around you. It means your garden stirs
        with mice eating
the seeds you planted. *You* or *she* or *I* are the slips

        we make in dreams,
flub our morning summary: *I was in the house watching
        the flood rise to your knees,*

and then I was you in the water and you were gone—
        If your mother calls out in a dream,
it means you've been negligent

in your responsibilities, i.e., you're asleep
ten states away while a machine examines her brain
with its magnetic eye,

sees her dream of you crouching, replanting rows,
registers your faith
in the way the soil makes, from next-to-nothing,

something. This, which she showed you
year after year, appears on the screen as a line
of gray dots, a pattern

where it might otherwise be black.

It's unbecoming, my mother
said when I was little and lifted my skirt
    to disappear

behind it. Now, like the spider, I tote
    my bit of lead shot, metal coil
embedded where a baby could be. IUD in the hot

    pain of an interior
so interior I'd never felt it before. *It is unbecoming*—
    Like the spider, I struggled

under the eye of someone there to make sure
    I could bear it, absurd
grit of hurt, pinpoint contraction

    of potential becomings.
The clinic was ringed by tall eucalyptus, blooms
    like small toilet brushes, pink,

all over the ground. I envisioned the dollhouse
    whose tiny maid might scrub
with blossoms, spotless. *Some spotting*

    is normal. I tracked the flowers
across the lot to my car. There, too tender
    for the seat belt, I looked up

separately: *immaculate,* then *maculate,* then
             conception. The unsullied
ability to imagine something and slash

          or bring it into existence—the windshield
wipers swiped away the flowers, the seat belt light
          flashed, as I drove, its warning.

We were assigned, at thirteen, dolls
        that cried, required
our care for days: Baby Think It Overs.

        They had a chip to note the time
it took to plug into their keyhole backs a plastic key.
        We had to hold it

in to quell the crying. The dolls' heads
        were hollow. You could press
at the nose, leave the face caved in, a comfort

        to make it less
babyish, though some girls rocked or rubbed,
        absentmindedly, their backs

where the battery pack hatch
        hid under bright fabric.
Who's to say if it worked? Some girls

        you saw in the high school halls
and then they were gone. I knew what it was
        to have a doll—I had the copy

of myself I made in the lonely canyon I lived in
        to talk to. I didn't need
eighth grade. These days, though, I wonder

        what it will feel like
to be transformed into a door through which someone,
        squalling, will arrive—perhaps

the better lesson is not to care
        for an object,
but to practice being made into one,

        to meditate long on the turnstile,
the vending machine, the fancy coffeemaker
        that grinds its own beans,

pulls from its own
        reservoir of water.

Before you know what it is, it is
a meringue, contained by its billowing
        shape, some strange mushroom

puffing up in the sunset. Then, though, the smoke
        becomes the air, a sudden way to see
the imperceptible, reminder of the contract

        between breath and everything else.
Someone helped me pick out the perfect shade
        of foundation, showed me the cloud

of setting powder. There are so many mysteries
        the Internet solves
with its videos. When all I thought about

        was how sick she was, I heard
the baby clock going off, ceaseless soft bell.
        Not an alarm, more like the signal

that class is done, some kind of end.
        Time for a transformation! Hours, then
I spent in front of the mirror, holding

        on to myself, hence the interest
in the exact right shade. The hot orange ribbon
        of flame prefers

to chew its way uphill, so the fire crew
        just waits at the top of the ridge,
fights it there. At dark, my brother and father

        return sooty and thirsty.
A portion of the canyon singes black, which means
        a million more larkspur come spring.

In the event of a fly or beetle thrust headlong
        into a web, the silk turns
momentum to heat, releases gently,

        does not sling the creature
back into the air. Silk, a miracle: able
        to absorb kinetic energy

better than anything man-made. The military
        wants this material for bulletproof
body armor, but silk farms

        fail—the spiders
attack each other, fight to the death.
        They are territorial, need

their own small realm, make themselves
        economically inefficient.
What we want is to feel

        like we're wearing nothing, wanting
for nothing, our territories bleeding
        into bigger blotches,

like wine dripped on a dress slip. This silk
        our body sees
as kindred—this world we feel

        exceptional in.

When I was young
and dumb or foolish, I felt what many girls feel,
        which was terror

that I could become an accidental
        receptacle, warm incubator
of someone else.

        Part of the fear
was from what grows, hijacks
        the controls:

that loss of jurisdiction
        over my own jewely
interior. I knifed and knifed through

        the plastic mesh this morning
to extricate a long gray snake, hopelessly tangled
        in garden netting. It didn't

want help; it menaced, shook its tail like a rattler,
        though it wasn't. I thought to call
animal control, but the language didn't sit right—

        control to free
the creature from what kept it. I was
        supposed to be calling myself

a woman all this time I was saying *girl*. I know my body
        tries to turn the IUD
into a person, and thwarts and thwarts

itself, a little battle
        in the dim inside of me.

Terrifically alone, in tulips
        the rain made of the South China Sea
I swam to a tiny island scrimmed with washed-up coral

        and purple shells.
I saw how many perfect ones
        awaited me. Giddy,

ashore, I pawed through them, straightened up
        only when my hands were full. It was
like realizing I'd put on someone else's jacket

        by accident. The joy
was not my own. It was my mother who could never leave
        a beach without a box of shells—

she found the hard armor of small creatures
        irresistible. Eerie and perfect,
the certainty that the delight I felt was hers,

        grafted onto me, sewn into me.

The moon pulls the ocean and the moon snail
            envelops its prey, say
a clam or mussel, and, with its built-in drill

            and shell solvent,
makes a small round hole through which it eats.
            Makes of the shell a pendant

to string onto a necklace, talisman, inadvertent
            monument to hunger, or
is it fear—

The round bottle cap of skull, pulled up
to expose the *dura mater,* was said to release the demons
of those acting strangely, those suffering

from invisible forces. To bring back from the dead
those thought to be dead,
e.g., the severely concussed. If it worked,

the disc of bone was worn to ward
off whatever had clamored to be released, whatever
had interfered—

my mother's talisman: asphalt
embedded in the skin of her temple,
smattering of gray dots, worn to repel

the earth, to undo her ever-after
desire to close the distance
between it and her—it didn't

work, or maybe it was working all the time.
Who knows the other version
of the story? The one where a nurse attends

to her patient instead
of evacuating, who, as the hurricane washes
the town into the sea, cleans the gravel

out of my mother's head, makes sure she knows
the year, the president, the names
of her children.

The *dura mater*, hard
mother, thick outer layer: there to protect
        the thing that is the thing

that makes you you, there to carry blood
        from the brain to the heart,
from the word for *tough*, for *coarse*. Of course,

        imperfect. Post trauma,
blood collects between the *dura* and *arachnoid*
        maters, memory

goes: the past is what gets flooded from you
        when blood comes
between the spider mother and the mother

        that lasts, the *durable* one. Some
have talk radio or science. Some have horoscopes,
        economics. Some study the world

with etymology—language, the sole
        mediator between the self
and what might be

        thought of as the *non-self*—

Memory loss, some think, is evolutionary,
        that women who forget
everything, save

        their infant, ensure
survival. My mother, bored, left the hospital
        for the library, read there waiting

for her labor to begin. I narrowly missed being born
        into a building of books,
and instead suffered into the regular light

        of the hospital
with the other babies, each of us
        tugging our mothers'

field of vision shut, like the mouth
        of a drawstring purse.
As with all families, there comes a role

        reversal. Life's weird curriculum, lesson
too late to do any good. I try to supply
        the word *geranium* and the aperture

of my mind contracts to a small spotlight
        in which my mother
waters something flouncy and red. I'm reminded

        of wearing a Halloween costume, eye to a little
misplaced hole, view of the ground
        ahead of me. The bare

minimum of information
        needed to keep walking.

The snail, so human, recoils
       into its privacy, becomes a shape,
unavailable, comforting

       in the palm, like a stone.
The brain of the snail has a ganglion like a person's
       but bigger, slower, easier

to observe: an ideal nervous system to study
       under the microscope,
though with what we call the *naked eye*

       we can see ourselves
hiding the way the snail does, our whole
       set of fears and hunger

spooled up inside us.

A web: the most practical art.
Whatever the world offers in the way
        of sustenance snares

in those careful lines. Every morning,
        the spider sets to: finds
a way to string from branch

        to house, from solid thing
to solid thing, in order to stand on what
        looks like air, waiting. It's hard

to believe. By this, I mean we forget
        there is a space
between what has been said and what

        has been said,
where we might wait for our survival
        to be furnished.

I know she followed the nerves
        with her mind's eye—the flaring
impulses, like bright drops of dew down a silk thread

        from the brain to the shape
of a word within the mouth, to the cup brought to the lips, rip
        of silk, the dial-down of the light dimmer—

I'm doing it again. Hopeful deployment of words I like,
        making the nothing into a picture, but what
can I use the picture for? A dream

        to fill the stretch of months
in which she practiced keeping
        the diagnosis unsaid, held it close.

A preparation, perhaps
        she practiced lying
very still, practiced dying—

How is she? I don't say *I am afraid to hear*
   of something final, some certain
end date. *How* is she—I employ a polite

   veer-away: *She remains*
in high spirits. Or *Her lemon tree is blooming.*
   Or *Her dog excels in agility class.*

Which is true: her dog, at long last, can be coaxed
   into the narrow tunnel
with one cloth end collapsed,

   a thing designed for this sole purpose:
to appear to have no exit. No dog
   likes the way it looks.

One way to do it is to army-crawl in, yourself,
   a treat in your pocket.
Certain dogs will follow and certain dogs will meet you

   at the other end.
But my mother could not crawl, could not
   show the dog

it was possible to enter the dead end,
   and find a way out.
I don't know what she did, but I watch now

   how she can say *In,* and point.
And the dog crawls in.

ACKNOWLEDGMENTS

I BEAR A DEBT OF GRATITUDE TO MANY PEOPLE WHO HELPED MAKE THIS book what it is. To my teachers, whose wisdom and support I continue to benefit from, particularly Marianne Boruch, Don Platt, Eavan Boland, and Alan Shapiro, thank you. To my intelligent and thoughtful friends who read pieces or drafts of this book along the way, Matt Morton, Shamala Gallagher, Jacques Rancourt, and Corey Van Landingham, you are invaluable. I am lucky to know you.

To Monica Youn, for choosing this book for the National Poetry Series, I am grateful for this honor. To Dan Halpern, for your fostering of this book and for everything you've done in support of poetry, thank you. To the wonderful people at Ecco, especially, Gabriella Doob, I appreciate your work and attention.

Lastly, my deepest gratitude to my parents; I owe my art to the life you made for me. And to Jacob, with love and respect, for things too numerous to list.

CREDITS

AGNI:
"[The *dura mater,* hard]," "[The round bottle cap of skull,
pulled up]," "[Perhaps it wasn't her head hitting the rocks]"

Beloit Poetry Journal:
"Nervous System" appeared as "[It's the one where the wolf],"
"[Her blood so thin when they drew it],"
"[How is she? I don't say *I am afraid to hear*],"
"[A web: the most practical art.]"

Field:
"[After a head trauma, distance]," "[I am at the ballet, watching a
woman]," "[I know she followed the nerves]"

From the Fishouse:
"[I started out looking]," "[I was taught the lyric is a song],"
"[Up early for the long drive home, I become]"

The Iowa Review:
"[Terrifically alone, in tulips]," "[So out-in-the-middle-of-nowhere,
that there]" appeared as "[Spiders have what is called book lungs]"

New Ohio Review:
"[I was taught the lyric is a song]," "[We played a game on the bus
that took us]," "[To dream of a storm]"

32 Poems:
"[Up early for the long drive home, I become],"
"[She studied snails]"

NATIONAL POETRY SERIES WINNERS

THE NATIONAL POETRY SERIES WAS ESTABLISHED IN 1978 TO ENSURE the publication of five collections of poetry annually through five participating publishers. The Series is funded annually by Amazon Literary Partnership, Betsy Community Fund, the Gettinger Family Foundation, Bruce Gibney, HarperCollins Publishers, Stephen King, Lannan Foundation, Newman's Own Foundation, Anna and Olafur Olafsson, the O.R. Foundation, the PG Family Foundation, the Poetry Foundation, Elise and Steven Trulaske, and the National Poetry Series Board of Directors.

THE NATIONAL POETRY SERIES WINNERS OF 2018 OPEN COMPETITION

Nervous System, Rosalie Moffett
Chosen by Monica Youn for Ecco

Eyes Bottle Dark with a Mouthful of Flowers, Jake Skeets
Chosen by Kathy Fagan for Milkweed Editions

Fear of Description, Daniel Poppick
Chosen by Brenda Shaughnessy for Penguin Books

It's Not Magic, Jon Sands
Chosen by Richard Blanco for Beacon Press

Valuing, Christopher Kondrich
Chosen by Jericho Brown for University of Georgia Press